The Problem With
Human Rights Law

The Problem With Human Rights Law

Is it out of control?
Who is responsible?
What is the solution?

Michael Arnheim

CIVITAS

First Published March 2015

Copyright © Dr Michael Arnheim 2015

Civitas
55 Tufton Street
London SW1P 3QL

email: books@civitas.org.uk

ISBN 978-1-906837-69-3

Independence: Civitas: Institute for the Study of Civil
Society is a registered educational charity (No. 1085494)
and a company limited by guarantee (No. 04023541).
Civitas is financed from a variety of private sources
to avoid over-reliance on any single or small group
of donors.

All publications are independently refereed. All the
Institute's publications seek to further its objective of
promoting the advancement of learning. The views
expressed are those of the authors, not of the Institute.

Designed and typeset by
lukejefford.com

Printed in Great Britain by
Berforts Group Ltd
Stevenage, SGI 2BH

Contents

Author

Dr Michael Arnheim (or 'Doctor Mike', as he is commonly known) is a practising London barrister and sometime fellow of St John's College, Cambridge. He has written 15 published books to date, including *The Handbook of Human Rights Law, Principles of the Common Law* and *The US Constitution for Dummies.*

Michael Arnheim entered Johannesburg's Witwatersrand University at the age of 16, taking a first class BA in history and classics at the age of 19, first class honours at 20 and an MA with distinction at the age of 21.

He then went up to St John's College, Cambridge, on a scholarship. There he was awarded a PhD in record time and it was published by the Oxford University Press. He was subsequently elected a fellow of St John's College, where he continued to do research and teach classics, especially ancient history.

At the age of 31 he was appointed a full professor and head of the department of classics back at his old university in South Africa. After some years in that position he returned to Britain, where he was called to the Bar by Lincoln's Inn in 1988 and continues to practise as a London barrister.

Introduction

There is a serious problem with human rights law. In my *Handbook of Human Rights Law*, originally published in 2004, I expressed the view that human rights law had been hijacked by a number of special interest groups, made up notably of convicted killers, terrorist suspects, asylum seekers and illegal immigrants. Before offering a solution to this problem it is necessary to identify its cause. Critics are too quick to blame the European Court of Human Rights for the expansion of the scope of the convention rights, when the evidence shows that it is actually the UK domestic courts which are largely responsible for this, together with a supine attitude on the part of successive British governments.

There are two Europes and at least three bills of rights. The European Convention on Human Rights (ECHR) is not directly connected with the European Union (EU) but is a product of a completely different body known as the Council of Europe, based in Strasbourg. (Strasbourg is itself confusing, because it is also the main seat of the parliament of the European Union, whose court, the European Court of Justice [ECJ], has its seat in Luxembourg!)

The Council of Europe is actually the oldest and largest extant European body, dating from 1949 and boasting no fewer than 47 members right across the continent, including Russia and even Turkey. Yet most people have never heard of it. It is essentially an umbrella body promoting co-operation between its member states, especially in the field of human rights.

The ECHR was drafted under the auspices of the Council of Europe in 1950, just five years after the end of World War II. Among its provisions was the establishment of a European Court of Human Rights (ECtHR) sitting in Strasbourg together with a preliminary tribunal known as the European Commission of Human Rights.

The UK was a founder member of the Council of Europe and one of the first signatories to the ECHR. This enabled UK residents to take cases to the European Commission of Human Rights, provided they had exhausted all domestic remedies first. The Commission acted as a filter. If it decided that a case was well founded, it would refer the case to the ECtHR on the applicant's behalf. In 1998 the procedure was streamlined by abolishing the Commission and enabling individuals to take cases directly to the ECtHR (still providing they had exhausted all domestic remedies) without the prior consent of their national government, which had previously been required.

In 1998 another important development took place as far as the UK was concerned, when (most but not the whole of) the ECHR was incorporated into the Human Rights Act 1998 and thereby became part of UK law, which meant that it could be invoked before the UK courts, which had never been possible before.

The Problem

There has been growing dissatisfaction with judicial decisions on human rights issues in certain quarters, which has developed into a clamour for a 'UK Bill of Rights'. In October 2014 the Conservative Party issued a strategy paper titled 'Protecting Human Rights in the UK'.[1] Under the heading 'The Case for Change' we read: 'Over the past 20 years, there have been significant developments which have undermined public confidence in the human rights framework in the UK, and which make change necessary today.'

This Conservative paper attaches no blame to the convention itself, saying: 'The convention is an entirely sensible statement of the principles which should underpin any modern democratic nation.' Instead, it launches a two-pronged assault, first on the Strasbourg court (the ECtHR) and, secondly, on the UK's Human Rights Act 1998 (HRA), the attack on which is in several parts. I will look at each of these accusations in turn.

1. The European Court of Human Rights

The ECtHR is blamed for adopting the doctrine or principle that the convention is a 'living instrument', and for then using this doctrine 'to expand convention rights into new areas, and certainly beyond what the framers of the convention had in mind when they signed up to it' –

amounting to 'mission creep'. The paper adds: 'There is mounting concern at Strasbourg's attempts to overrule decisions of our democratically elected parliament and overturn the UK courts' careful applications of convention rights.'

False premise

There is a serious mistake here. Although Strasbourg is undoubtedly guilty of 'mission creep', the UK judges have *not* taken a different line from Strasbourg. Instead, they have religiously followed Strasbourg's line in almost every case. In the words of the former lord chancellor and architect of the Human Rights Act, Lord Irvine of Lairg, the domestic courts of the UK have proceeded 'on the false premise that they are bound (or as good as bound) to follow any clear decision of the ECtHR which is relevant to a case before them'.[2]

I have to say that I am in full agreement with Lord Irvine's analysis, which focuses particularly on HRA section 2(1)(a), reading: 'A court or tribunal determining a question which has arisen in connection with a convention right must take into account any – (a) judgment, decision, declaration or advisory opinion of the European Court of Human Rights.' As Lord Irvine points out:

> 'Take account of' is not the same as 'follow', 'give effect to' or 'be bound by'. Parliament, if it had wished, could have used any of these formulations. It did not. The meaning of the provision is clear. The judges are not bound to follow the Strasbourg court: they must decide the case for themselves.

Yet, with very few exceptions, the UK courts have regarded themselves as being obliged to follow Strasbourg.

'Starkest example'

As 'the starkest example' of this wrong approach Lord Irvine singled out the House of Lords decision in *AF v Secretary of State for the Home Department*,[3] a case about control orders issued under the Prevention of Terrorism Act 2005. The appellants contended that their right to a fair hearing under ECHR Article 6 had been violated by the judge's reliance on secret material not disclosed to the appellants. In Lord Irvine's words: 'The House unanimously allowed the appeal, and in doing so clearly proceeded on the premise that it was obliged to do so.'

Lord Hoffmann, who is himself not uncritical of the Strasbourg court, said:

> *A v United Kingdom* requires these appeals to be allowed. I do so with very considerable regret, because I think that the decision of the ECtHR was wrong and that it may well destroy the system of control orders which is a significant part of this country's defences against terrorism. Nevertheless, I think that your Lordships have no choice but to submit. It is true that section 2(1)(a) of the Human Rights Act 1998 requires us only to 'take into account' decisions of the ECHR. As a matter of our domestic law, we could take the decision in *A v United Kingdom* into account but nevertheless prefer our own view. But the United Kingdom is bound by the convention, as a matter of international law, to accept the decisions of the ECtHR on its interpretation. To reject such a decision would almost certainly put this country in breach of the international obligation which it accepted when it acceded to the convention. I can see no advantage in your Lordships doing so.

Lord Rodger of Earlsferry made the same point even more briefly:

> Even though we are dealing with rights under a United Kingdon statute, in reality, we have no choice: *Argentoratum locutum, iudicium finitum* – Strasbourg has spoken, the case is closed.

Besides disagreeing with the sentiment expressed here, I would amend the Latin to read: *Argentorato locuto, iudicium finitum.*

Lord Irvine's comment is direct and authoritative:

> I beg to differ. Section 2 of the HRA means that the domestic Court *always* has a choice. Further, not only is the domestic Court entitled to make the choice, its statutory duty under s.2 *obliges* it to confront the question whether or not the relevant decision of the ECtHR is sound in principle and should be given effect domestically. Simply put, the domestic Court *must* decide the case for itself. (Emphasis added)

It is worth remarking that the whole control order system was in fact introduced only because the preventive detention regime brought in by parliament after 9/11 was struck down by the House of Lords (as a court) in *A (FC) v Secretary of State for the Home Department*,[4] resulting in a situation where there were certain foreign nationals who could neither be prosecuted nor deported, thus forcing the government to resort to control orders based to some extent on secret evidence, which required a derogation from ECHR Article 5 (right to liberty), which could be claimed only 'in time of war or other public emergency threatening the life of the nation' (ECHR Article 15(1)). But the government was thwarted here once again. Lord Hoffmann predicted:

> This is a nation which has been tested in adversity, which has survived physical destruction and catastrophic loss of life. I do not underestimate the

ability of fanatical groups of terrorists to kill and destroy, but they do not threaten the life of the nation. Whether we would survive Hitler hung in the balance, but there is no doubt that we shall survive Al Qaeda… Terrorist violence, serious as it is, does not threaten our institutions of government or our existence as a civil community. (§96)

This optimistic prognostication raises two questions. First, on what basis did Lord Hoffman come to this conclusion? But secondly, and more importantly, is this not a political question which falls squarely within the domain of the executive? It should be noted that Strasbourg had not adjudicated on this question at all.

The government had been pushed from pillar to post and was now in a most invidious position in regard to persons whom the government could neither prosecute nor deport. But why could these people not be deported? Section 3(5)(a) of the Immigration Act 1971 (as amended) provides: 'A person who is not a British citizen is liable to deportation from the United Kingdom if (a) the Secretary of State deems his deportation to be conducive to the public good.' This can only be a *political* question to be decided by the executive, and not a *legal* question for the courts.

This takes us back to one of the many pernicious decisions of the ECtHR, which has been slavishly followed by the UK courts: *Chahal v UK*,[5] which decided that it was a violation of ECHR Article 3 to deport a foreign national if there was a real risk that he would be subjected to treatment contrary to ECHR Article 3 at the hands of the receiving state. Is this really what Article 3 says? Not at all. Here is what Article 3 says: 'No one shall be subjected to torture or to inhuman or degrading treatment or punishment.' Subjected to torture etc by whom? The whole of the ECHR is addressed to the 'High Contracting Parties', ie the states which signed it. So, what Article 3 is saying is that the signatory states must not subject anyone to torture etc. Therefore, the UK, as a signatory state, must not torture anybody. But where does it say that the UK must also be responsible for the treatment received by someone in another country after being deported from the UK? Nowhere.

This is a huge unwarranted extension of Article 3 by the Strasbourg court – and followed by the UK courts without exception. Of course, if a person is deported from one signatory state to another, then the deportee is protected from torture etc by the obligation of the receiving state under Article 3. But, if the deportation is to a non-convention state, it is an infringement of the sovereign rights of the deporting state to make that state responsible for the treatment accorded the deportee in the receiving state.

The whole series of cases in which the government was repeatedly thwarted in its attempts to keep terrorism at bay was indeed based on Strasbourg jurisprudence – but Strasbourg jurisprudence closely followed and applied by the domestic courts. The obvious question that arises from the UK domestic courts' reluctance to depart from Strasbourg decisions is: Why? It surely cannot be because the judges have misunderstood the meaning of the common phrase 'take into account'.

'With very considerable regret'

Lord Hoffmann's decision in the AF case to follow Strasbourg (taken, in his own words, 'with very considerable regret' as he believed it to be wrong and damaging to the UK's defence against terrorism) was evidently based on ECHR Article 46, providing that the signatory states 'undertake to abide by the final judgment of the Court (of Human Rights) in any case to which they are a party'. Here again Lord Irvine strikes home:

> My own view is that excessive preoccupation with this consideration has led the Courts into error. A judge's concern for the UK's foreign policy and its standing in international relations can never justify disregarding the clear statutory direction which s.2 of the HRA provides.

The point is that matters of foreign policy are the concern of the Executive government and not of the courts, which are primarily bound by domestic law.

Rights v rights

The second reason which appears to make UK domestic courts follow Strasbourg as closely as they do – and sometimes even to out-Strasbourg Strasbourg – is the mistake of failing to recognise that human rights cases concern human rights *on both sides*. Cases involving terrorism or national security, for example, are commonly described by the courts as requiring a balance to be struck between human rights and national security, or between the individual right to liberty and the public interest. Putting it like this is misleading. Abstract terms like 'national security' and 'the public interest' tend to pale by comparison with 'the rights of the individual'. Yet, 'national security' and 'the public interest' actually refer to the *human rights* of thousands or even millions of *individuals*. Preventing the government from detaining or deporting potentially dangerous individuals may result in the violation of the individual rights to liberty or even to life of thousands of law-abiding citizens. And this needs to be spelt out in each and every relevant case.

'Political correctness'

A more disquieting reason for the UK domestic courts' tendency to trot along with the Strasbourg line is that this 'politically correct' approach happens to chime in with the individual political views of a number of the domestic judges. The traditional view that judges are politically neutral is simply naïve. Referring to public law cases in general, that acute observer of the relationship between the judiciary and the executive, Professor J.A.G. Griffith, remarked: 'The idea that judges can be politically neutral in such cases has never been true.'[6] Judges have political views just like anybody else, which cannot simply be put to one side while they are sitting on the bench. And most human rights cases have a political dimension. All that has changed over the years is the judges' predilections. The famous liberal American Supreme Court Justice Felix Frankfurter was a model of judicial restraint, because he believed that the judiciary should not interfere with decisions taken by democratically elected bodies or institutions. 'Political correctness', however, unfortunately tends to breed judicial activism, or even judicial supremacism. An (unintentionally) amusing example of this was provided by a staunch academic protagonist of judicial activism, Professor Ronald Dworkin, who opined: 'I cannot imagine what argument might be thought to show that legislative decisions about rights are inherently more likely to be right than judicial decisions.'[7] It evidently did not occur to Dworkin that there is a very obvious argument, namely that, unlike judicial decisions, legislative decisions are *democratic*.

More and more English judges are now starting to pooh-pooh the age-old British constitutional principle of the sovereignty of parliament and the rule that legislation and policy decisions are no-go areas for the courts. Even Lord Sumption, who has the reputation of being a conservative justice, dismissed Lord Diplock's well-known distinction between politics and law with the disdainful comment: 'Like many of Lord Diplock's more oracular pronouncements, this is not so much an answer as a restatement of the problem. Where does law end and policy begin?'[8] In practice the borderline is not as difficult to detect as this seems to imply. And it must also be remembered that a decision on which side of the divide a particular issue falls is itself *legislation*, which is for parliament and not for the courts to decide.

2. The Human Rights Act

The HRA is a mixed bag. The Conservative paper is certainly correct to single out section 3(1) for special condemnation. But an even more pernicious section, which has escaped the paper's notice is section 6(1), which provides: 'It is unlawful for a public authority to act in a way which is incompatible with a convention right.' Section 4(6)(a), on the other hand, provides expressly that even if a UK law is declared by a court to be 'incompatible' with a particular convention right, that 'does not affect the validity, continuing operation or enforcement of the provision' in question. And there is of course section 2, which only requires the domestic courts to take Strasbourg rulings 'into account' – though, as we have seen, the UK domestic courts have very largely chosen to regard themselves as bound by Strasbourg jurisprudence.

'Labour's Human Rights Act undermines the role of the UK courts in deciding human rights issues in this country'

The Conservative paper claims: 'Section 2 of the HRA requires UK courts to "take into account" rulings of the Strasbourg Court when they are interpreting convention rights. This means problematic Strasbourg jurisprudence is often being applied in UK law.' This misses the point made so cogently by Lord Irvine that the UK courts have *chosen* to follow Strasbourg, which they are not obliged to do. Indeed, it is their duty to depart from Strasbourg jurisprudence when they consider it to be wrong. But they don't – except in a very small number of cases, in some of which the domestic courts have actually gone further than Strasbourg in extending the scope of convention rights! A trawl through human rights cases of recent years makes it clear that the UK courts treat themselves as bound by Strasbourg although they aren't.

The Conservative paper singles out proportionality for particular condemnation. Proportionality is indeed a European concept (although, while wrongly attributed to Strasbourg, it actually comes from that *other* European court, namely the European Court of Justice, the court of the European Union sitting in Luxembourg). But, so supine has the UK government and parliament become that proportionality was even allowed to creep into UK primary legislation, like, for example, paragraph 9(6) of Schedule 7 to the Counter-Terrorism Act 2008. Proportionality is now so embedded in English law – by decisions of the *domestic* courts – that it would be very difficult if not impossible to eradicate it.

But what exactly is wrong with the principle of proportionality? The Conservative paper objects that 'the application of this doctrine has led judges to question whether provisions of legislation and decisions of public authorities are "proportional" to their objectives, which can amount to an essentially political evaluation of different policy considerations.' Here the Conservative paper does indeed have a point, but it is once again misconstrued. For judges to make political decisions is a no-no. So what impels them to do so? Does the principle of proportionality confront them as a ghostly apparition and force them to stray into this forbidden territory? Not exactly. When judges overstep their powers in this way it is they and they alone who make the decision to do so. And what does parliament do when this happens? In most cases, nothing at all. Parliament certainly has the right to reverse the effect of a judicial decision by means of legislation, but it has very rarely done so. What is needed is a pre-emptive remedy stopping judges from making decisions which they have no authority to make in the first place.

'Labour's Human Rights Act undermines the sovereignty of parliament and democratic accountability'

The most pernicious provision of the HRA, which is not mentioned in the Conservative paper, is section 6(1): 'It is unlawful for a public authority to act in a way which is incompatible with a convention right.' This evidently gives this important power to the courts, which enables them to declare government acts 'unlawful'. It is important to note that parliament is not regarded as a public authority for these purposes. So section 6 does not give any court the right to strike down parliamentary legislation. Nevertheless, this pernicious section must certainly be repealed post haste.

The Conservative paper is clearly right to object to HRA section 3(1), which provides that: 'So far as it is possible to do so, primary legislation and subordinate legislation must be read and given effect in a way which is compatible with the convention rights.' The Conservative paper comments:

> There are cases in which, due to this rule, UK courts have gone to artificial lengths to change the meaning of legislation so that it complies with their interpretation of convention rights, most often following Strasbourg's interpretation, even if this is inconsistent with parliament's intention when enacting the relevant legislation.

But, if a domestic court goes to 'artificial lengths' to read down domestic legislation so as to comply with Strasbourg, who is to blame for that? Once again, this is a decision freely taken by the domestic court concerned.

In order to avoid this situation, what the domestic court should do is to avail itself of the machinery of HRA section 4, which is specifically intended to safeguard the sovereignty of parliament. Section 4 provides that, if a court 'is satisfied' that a piece of legislation is incompatible with a convention right, it may (*not* must) make a declaration of incompatibility. But, as we have seen, section 4(6) makes it clear that a declaration of incompatibility 'does not affect the validity, continuing operation or enforcement' of the legislative provision in question.

'Labour's Human Rights Act goes far beyond the UK's obligations under the convention'

This objection is not at all clear. But the Conservative paper then homes in on a comparison with Germany: 'The German Constitutional Court for example ruled that if there is a conflict between the German Basic Law and the ECHR, then the Basic Law prevails over the convention. The Human Rights Act provides no such domestic protection in the UK.' This is only partly correct. The point is that Germany has a written constitution (or Basic Law), which has higher law status. The ECHR has been incorporated into German law, but only as an ordinary statute. So, in the event of a conflict, the German Constitution trumps the ECHR.

In the UK the position is that no statute is entrenched or has higher law status. The attempt on the part of certain UK judges to suggest that there is a two-tier system of statutes and that the ECHR (insofar as it is incorporated into the HRA) has higher law status is just simply wrong. Such a major decision would require legislation, which is entrusted to parliament, not to the courts. But even parliament could not really make such a decision, because entrenching a particular law or clause would fly in the face of the fundamental constitutional principle that no parliament can bind its successors – a principle which is actually implicit in the principle of the sovereignty of parliament. So the position of the ECHR in the UK is essentially the same as its position in Germany. In both, the ECHR has the status of an ordinary statute. Once again, therefore, we find that it is the UK courts, not Strasbourg, which must be blamed.

To sum up, therefore, on the points made in the Conservative paper:

● The Strasbourg court is indeed guilty of 'mission creep', but the blame for this reaching the UK rests squarely on the shoulders of the UK domestic courts, who are not only *not* obliged to follow Strasbourg but have a positive duty to depart from

Strasbourg jurisprudence and follow English law whenever there is a clash between the two.

● The HRA does not undermine the role of the UK domestic courts, which are never obliged to follow Strasbourg rulings.

● So far from undermining the sovereignty of parliament, the HRA actually safeguards it – with the serious exception of section 6(1) and also of section 3(1), both of which certainly need to be repealed.

The Conservatives' plan for change

In view of the Conservative paper's misdiagnosis of the true nature of the problem, its suggested solution is inevitably seriously flawed. I will just look at its main proposals before setting out my alternative solution. The paper says that the planned Conservative reforms will mean that:

● *'The European Court of Human Rights is no longer binding over the UK Supreme Court'*

The Strasbourg court can't bind the UK courts even now. The reason it looks as though it can is because the UK courts themselves choose to follow Strasbourg rulings (see above). In *R (Ullah) v Special Adjudicator* (2004) UKHL 236, Lord Bingham held that no national court should 'without strong reason dilute or weaken the effect of Strasbourg case law'. This is not in keeping with HRA section 2, which only requires the domestic courts to 'take account of' Strasbourg decisions. It is disquieting that Lord Bingham's dictum is quoted as authoritative on the UK Supreme Court's own website – yet a further example of the fact that the decision to follow Strasbourg is one made by the domestic courts themselves.

● *'The European Court of Human Rights is no longer able to order a change in UK law and becomes an advisory body'*

This is another product of misunderstanding. In fact, the strict legal position is that the Strasbourg court cannot order a change in UK law even now. In practice, however, a finding by Strasbourg in favour of an applicant has been unnecessarily taken as binding by the UK domestic courts and has generally been followed by the capitulation of the UK government, which has just meekly applied the Strasbourg ruling.

● *'There is a proper balance between rights and responsibilities in UK law'*

In fact, ECHR Articles 8, 9, 10 and 11 already contain qualifications allowing the convention rights concerned to be subjected to limitations 'necessary in a democratic society', although Strasbourg has defined 'necessity' very narrowly, requiring 'a pressing social need' and proof that the limitation is 'proportionate to the legitimate aim pursued' – which as usual the UK courts have simply followed. Even more important is the neglected point I made above, which even the Conservative paper fails to recognise, and that is that the balance is not between 'individual rights' and 'the public interest', to which 'responsibilities' may be added, but between the rights of one individual and the individual rights of thousands or even millions of individuals, which is a more accurate way of describing it from a human rights perspective.

However, adding a list of responsibilities to the legislation would certainly do no harm.

The Conservative paper goes on to identify 'two basic legal facts' on which its proposals are based:

- *There is no formal requirement for our Courts to treat the Strasbourg Court as creating legal precedent for the UK*

  Here the Conservative paper gets into a muddle again, by saying: 'Such a requirement was introduced in the Human Rights Act, and it is for Parliament to decide whether or not it should continue.' As I have emphasised above, all that the HRA requires is that the UK courts 'take account of' Strasbourg decisions, which therefore are not binding precedents as far as the UK courts are concerned. It is the UK courts themselves who have chosen to treat Strasbourg decisions as binding on themselves. But it certainly can do no harm for parliament to clarify the true legal position in amending legislation.

- *'In all matters related to our international commitments, parliament is sovereign'*

  This is a fundamental principle, which certainly needs to be stressed. Judges should be concerned, and concerned only, to reach the right decision according to UK domestic law without considerations of the UK's international relations, which is a matter for parliament and the executive. This approach would have saved Lord Hoffmann in the *AF* case from regretfully making a decision which he knew was wrong – because of his concern about the UK's treaty obligations under ECHR Article 46. Lord Irvine's point cited above is relevant here: the UK's foreign policy and international relations are a matter for the government, not for the courts, whose prime responsibility is to UK domestic law and not to the UK's international treaty obligations.

Key Objectives

The Conservative paper goes on to outline 'the key objectives' of the proposed new Bill of Rights, as follows:

- *'Repeal Labour's Human Rights Act'*

  This I believe would be a serious mistake. As already indicated, the HRA certainly does contain some pernicious sections, notably sections 3 and 6, which must be repealed. But to repeal the whole Act would be throwing the baby out with the bathwater. The function of the HRA is to control the operation of the ECHR in the UK. So it can be used to lay down much clearer and more definite ground rules for the UK courts to use in applying the ECHR. Otherwise, if left to their own devices, for the reasons discussed above, the courts will continue their current practice of closely following Strasbourg.

- *'Put the text of the original Human Rights Convention into primary legislation'*

  This would also be a mistake. It is the result of a naïve belief that the ECHR on its own would be fine, if only it could be freed from the machinations of the Strasbourg court and the HRA. If it could only be prised loose from these, all would be well. This is a total fallacy. The ECHR comes with a lot of baggage – more than half a century of Strasbourg jurisprudence. As sure as eggs is eggs (to coin a phrase), the UK domestic courts will continue to follow Strasbourg's lead in interpreting and applying the ECHR. The reason that some UK judges have given for following Strasbourg is simply that the Strasbourg court is the one specifically charged by the Council of Europe to interpret and adjudicate on the ECHR. Of course, there is also another reason, as we have seen, why UK judges follow the Strasbourg line, and that is because it happens to chime in with their own political views. There is also another reason against making the whole original ECHR a piece of primary UK legislation, and that is that those parts of it that are already incorporated into the HRA already have that status but that, as the authors of the Conservative paper may not be aware, what is incorporated into the HRA is not the whole of the ECHR. Retaining the present structure may even give the government (through parliament) the opportunity to chop out a few more objectionable convention rights.

- *'Clarify the convention rights, to reflect a proper balance between rights and responsibilities'*

This makes sense but, as mentioned above, the obvious vehicle for such clarification is in an amended Human Rights Act, which could perhaps be rebranded as the Human Rights and Responsibilities Act (once it is passed).

- *'Break the formal link between between British courts and the European Court of Human Rights'*

The naïve faith rears its head again that, once freed from the obligation to take Strasbourg decisions 'into account', the UK courts will ignore Strasbourg jurisprudence in interpreting the convention rights. This, as we have seen, is a completely unrealistic expectation.

● *'End the ability of the European Court of Human Rights to force the UK to change the law'*

As mentioned above, even now Strasbourg cannot actually force the UK to change the law. In practice, however, it does have this power, for two reasons: first, the UK courts' usual close agreement with Strasbourg; and secondly, the British government's supineness in the face of Strasbourg decisions.

● *'Prevent our laws from being effectively rewritten through "interpretation"'*

Once again, we have the naïve statement that: 'In future, the UK courts will interpret legislation based upon its normal meaning and the clear intention of parliament, rather than having to stretch its meaning to comply with Strasbourg case-law.' Strasbourg has indeed extended the scope of convention rights in its decisions. But, as we have repeatedly seen, the UK courts have willingly followed Strasbourg's lead. And that will not change except under strong compulsion by parliament, and probably not even then.

My own suggested solution to the serious problems of human rights law will be found at the end of this pamphlet.

Case Studies

What follows are two case studies illustrating the present sorry state of human rights law and the British government's self-delusion.

Voting rights for prisoners

In October 2013 the appeals by two convicted killers against a denial of their right to vote were dismissed by the UK Supreme Court (UKSC). This decision was hailed by David Cameron as a 'a great victory for common sense'. In fact, however, there was general agreement among the justices that, in the words of Lord Clarke, 'this Court should follow the now settled jurisprudence in the Strasbourg court'.[9]

What then gave the Prime Minister the idea that the UKSC disagreed with Strasbourg? This was obviously because the Supreme Court was not prepared to find that either of the two appellants should be entitled to vote. In the words of Lady Hale: 'I have no sympathy at all for either of these appellants. I cannot envisage any law which the UK parliament might eventually pass on this subject which would grant either of them the right to vote.' (§99) But this does not mark a departure from Strasbourg. Indeed, it is clear from *Scoppola v Italy (No. 3)*[10] that the Strasbourg court itself *would* be prepared to accept the disqualification of killers sentenced to life imprisonment.

David Cameron is deluding himself if he thinks the UKSC supports the present blanket disqualification of all convicted prisoners. On the contrary, the UKSC stands four-square behind the Strasbourg court. In the words of Lord Sumption:

> (I)t would be neither wise not legally defensible for an English court to say that article 3 of the First Protocol has a meaning different from that which represents the settled view of the principal court charged with its interpretation, and different from that which will consequently apply in every other state party to the convention. (§138)

Wrong end of stick

As usual, the Conservative paper gets hold of the wrong end of the stick by claiming that the whole issue of voting rights had been 'deliberately excluded from the text of the convention'. It is true that the right to vote does not figure in the original version of the convention, but it did not take long for this right to be added, which was done by Article 3 of the First Protocol, which came into force as long ago as 1954. The UK was the very first member state to ratify it, on 3 November 1952 – when Churchill was prime minister. So it was certainly no belated afterthought – and the Strasbourg court cannot be blamed for expanding the scope of the convention by including it. It has been part of the convention for over sixty years! This, however, is a minor error on the part of the Conservative paper.

Article 3 of Protocol 1

What exactly does the protocol say? Protocol 1, Article 3 contains an undertaking by the member states 'to hold free elections at reasonable intervals by secret ballot, under conditions which will ensure the free expression of the opinion of the people in the choice of the legislature'. It stipulates secret ballot but does not specify who is to be allowed to vote or who, if anyone, is to be excluded from that right.

The position adopted by the Strasbourg court is that the blanket ban in UK law on the rights of convicted prisoners to vote in elections is incompatible with Article 3 of Protocol 1 of the ECHR, and it has ordered the UK to amend its law accordingly. This position has been expressed in a series of decisions since 2005, notably: *Hirst v UK (No 2)*[11]; *Greens v UK*[12], *Scoppola v Italy (No. 3)*[13], and *Firth v UK.*[14]

This does *not* mean that the Strasbourg court regards any restriction on prisoner voting rights as unacceptable. In a factsheet on 'Prisoners' right to vote' of October 2014 the Strasbourg court makes it clear that, despite the importance of voting rights: 'Nevertheless, the rights bestowed by Article 3 of Protocol No. 1 are not absolute.' Disqualification of convicted prisoners serving sentences of a specified length might well be acceptable, even if those prisoners are all disqualified automatically – as long as the disqualification does not amount to a blanket disqualification of *all* convicted prisoners serving *any* prison sentence irrespective of length.

Why Strasbourg is wrong

This can give little comfort to the British government. But is it correct? My own view is that it is not and that there are at least three good reasons for departing from the Strasbourg approach:

(a) The Strasbourg position is illogical

For one thing, Strasbourg's position can easily be impugned on the grounds of logic. In *Hirst* (No. 2) the Strasbourg court held that a blanket ban on all convicted prisoners serving sentences of *any* length was incompatible with the convention. But Strasbourg is nevertheless prepared to accept an automatic ban on convicted prisoners sentenced to more than a specified length of sentence and is apparently prepared to treat the choice of the length of sentence as covered by the so-called 'margin of appreciation', meaning that it will be left to the government of the relevant state to decide. It has to be recognised that the length of sentence selected, no matter what it is, will inevitably be arbitrary. However, the Strasbourg court in *Scoppola* was prepared to accept the Italian system, under which even a three-year prison sentence triggered an automatic ban on voting rights. But what about a six-month sentence? If the setting of the triggering length of sentence is left to the UK authorities, then even a one-week sentence should be acceptable. Or a one-day sentence. But we know from the Strasbourg jurisprudence that a rule that bans *all* convicted prisoners is not acceptable. Why? Why should a one-week sentence pass muster, but not a one-day sentence? There *is* no reason; and to make that distinction, which Strasbourg appears to be making in this area, must therefore be labelled illogical or even irrational.

(b) The current blanket ban has a democratic mandate

The UK parliament has been toying with two different amendments to the law giving the right to vote to prisoners sentenced to either less than 6 months' or less than four years' imprisonment. But neither of these amendments has passed into legislation, because parliament is implacably opposed to any wavering on this issue. This was made clear by the House of Commons on 11 February 2011 in a debate sponsored by senior backbenchers from both sides of the House, on a motion asserting that 'legislative decisions of this nature should be a matter for democratically elected lawmakers' and supporting 'the current situation under which no sentenced prisoner is able to vote except those imprisoned for contempt, default or on remand'. The House of Commons voted in favour of this motion by 234 votes to 22 (with both front benches abstaining).

This is in itself a strong argument for refusing to change the law, and it is further strengthened by public opinion. The view that 'no prisoners should be allowed to vote' was supported by 63 per cent of respondents in a YouGov poll taken in November 2012. It is not hard to see why this should be such a popular view.

(c) Law-breakers should not have a say on what the law should be

This links up with what is in my opinion the most powerful argument of all against allowing convicted prisoners to vote, which is that law-breakers should not have a say on what the law should be. The right to vote in parliamentary elections gives a voter the right to choose the candidate most likely to support legislation most favourable to that voter. There are a number of areas of law in which convicted prisoners have a common interest, including police powers, evidence, sentencing, drugs, and of course prison reform – a common interest which goes clean against the interests of justice and of society as a whole. It may be argued that, even if *all* convicted prisoners had the vote, their numbers would never be enough to influence legislation. There are two arguments against this. First, the issues which convicted prisoners are likely to favour are all already supported by 'liberal' parties of various hues. Take, for example, the legalisation of cannabis, which already has a sizable body of support behind it. Prisoner votes could possibly tip the balance in one or two marginal seats, resulting in the election of a few more MPs who favour the legalisation of cannabis. But, there is also a more fundamental argument against the right of prisoners to vote, and that is that imprisonment is meant to be a *punishment*, primarily through loss of liberty, and that loss of the right to vote should be seen as just another intrinsic facet of this punishment. At one time imprisonment resulted in complete 'civic death'. The loss of voting rights is not 'civic death' but just a small part of it, which might just possibly send a salutary message.

It is surprising to see how little notice has been taken of the argument that lawbreakers should have no say in law-making. The British government virtually capitulated in the Court of Appeal in the *Chester* case, as remarked by Lord Justice Laws: 'A signal feature of the case is that the Secretary of State concedes that Representation of the People Act 1983 s.3 is repugnant to Article 1 of the First Protocol.'[15] In other words, the government admitted that the disfranchisement of convicted prisoners amounted to a violation of the right to free elections – a completely unnecessary and indeed, in my opinion, wrong concession to make. Even the Strasbourg court held in *Scoppola* that the exclusion of convicted prisoners sentenced to more than three years' imprisonment did not violate the protocol.

In summing up the arguments on both sides in the Court of Appeal, Laws LJ in *Chester* mentioned only one that favoured exclusion: 'It might in particular be said that a person convicted of very grave crime has so far distanced himself from the values of civil society that it would be a travesty of justice to allow him to participate in its governance.' (§34) However, this misses the real point, which the Secretary of State evidently did not make. The point is not a philosophical argument about 'the values of civil society' but the down-to-earth practical point that a lawbreaker – and not only someone convicted of 'very grave crime' – should not be allowed to be involved in law-making, however indirectly.

In the UKSC in *Chester*, similarly, in enumerating the arguments on both sides, Lady Hale did not even mention the point that law-breakers should have no say on what the law should be. Instead, Lady Hale expressed the surprising view that: 'The arguments for and against their exclusion are quite finely balanced.'(§91) And the arguments enumerated by this justice largely favour prisoners' voting rights, including the remark that the blanket exclusion of prisoners from voting 'does not explain the purpose of the exclusion'. Yet, there is a very obvious purpose for the exclusion of convicted prisoners from voting – namely, once again, to prevent lawbreakers from influencing law-making. This in my opinion is an argument which trumps all arguments to the contrary, but which unfortunately was evidently not put forward on behalf of the government.

It is of course possible to raise objections to *any* disqualification of convicted prisoners, such as:

● *The arbitrary nature of the threshold for imprisonment.* The relevance of this point is dubious. The answer to this is that this threshold *will* inevitably be arbitrary to some extent and may also vary from one court to another, but a concession that there is *no* basis for imprisoning some offenders and not others is tantamount to a concession that the criminal justice system is in disarray. However, ironically perhaps, a blanket ban on all convicted prisoners is obviously less arbitrary than any other basis.

● *The arbitrary nature of any disqualification in terms of length of sentence.* A disqualification level of six months is just as arbitrary as one of four years or 20 years, but the Strasbourg court in *Scoppola* is evidently amenable to an automatic ban, as long as it does not cover *all* convicted prisoners, a position which, as we have seen, is illogical.

● *What about mental patients?* The objection is that there is no equivalent here to length of a prison sentence. So does that mean that all mental patients should be allowed to vote? Surely not. The simplest solution is just to leave the disqualification as already spelt out in section 3A of the Representation of the People Act 1983.

● *A democracy must protect minority as well as majority rights, and convicted prisoners are a minority not represented in parliament. So 'the views of the public and parliamentarians cannot be the end of the story'.*[16] It is hard to see the relevance of this objection to the question of prisoners' voting rights. In what sense do prisoners constitute a 'minority'? In my opinion, Lord Sumption has the better of the argument on this point in *Chester:*

> The protection of minorities is a necessary concern of any democratic constitution. But the present issue has nothing whatever to do with the protection of minorities. Prisoners belong to a minority only in the banal and legally irrelevant

sense that most people do not do the things which warrant imprisonment by due process of law. (§112)

Conclusion on voting rights

So far from the UK Supreme Court's supporting the blanket ban on prisoners' voting rights, as the government fondly believes, the court is four-square behind Strasbourg. What is also noteworthy is the government's legal representatives' unnecessary capitulation to Strasbourg in court.

Abu Qatada

This case study is the sorry saga of what might be called a yo-yo case, namely one that repeatedly goes one way and then another – and when lower courts even had the temerity to continue to follow a Strasbourg 'rule' after it had actually been declared to be wrong by the House of Lords. It also reveals the supineness of the Secretary of State in kowtowing to this same 'rule' in court in 2012, three years after it had been conclusively knocked on the head by the House of Lords. Besides being a yo-yo case it might also be called a ping-pong case, in which far too many appeals were permitted back and forth.

Abu Qatada (Omar Mahmoud Othman), a Jordanian national who was repeatedly imprisoned and released in the UK under anti-terrorism laws but was never charged with any crime, was eventually deported back to Jordan in July 2013. Some landmarks in the Abu Qatada saga are as follows:

- In 1999 he was sentenced *in absentia* by a Jordanian court to life imprisonment, to which a further 15 years were added in a subsequent trial held in Jordan in the year 2000.

- 2004: In dismissing Abu Qatada's appeal against detention without trial Mr Justice Collins, the then chairman of the Special Immigration Appeals Commission (SIAC), remarked that Abu Qatada had been 'concerned in the instigation of acts of international terrorism' and 'is a truly dangerous individual'.[17]

- 2006: In August 2005 Abu Qatada was served by the Home Secretary with a Notice of Intention to Deport him to Jordan. His appeal to the Special Immigration Appeals Commission (SIAC) was dismissed in a very detailed judgment running to 541 paragraphs.[18] His main objection to deportation was the danger that evidence used against him might have been obtained by torture. To counter this the UK government entered into a Memorandum of Understanding (MoU) with Jordan followed up by questions addressed to the Jordanian government relating specifically to the deportation of Abu Qatada. One of these questions was: 'Is confession evidence admissible even if the State Security Court have reason to believe that it was obtained by torture?' The clear and unequivocal answer to this given by the Jordanian government was 'no'.[19] The dismissal of Abu Qatada's appeal against deportation was based not only on the MoU and the questions, but even more so on this important general point of law: 'It is a fallacy to treat the ECHR obligation on the removing state as one which requires a guarantee, let alone a legally enforceable one, that there would be no risk at all of a breach of Article 3 in the receiving state.' (§494)

- 2008: Abu Qatada successfully appealed to the Court of Appeal, which roundly condemned the SIAC decision: 'It was not open to SIAC to conclude on the evidence that the risk of the total denial of justice that is represented by the use of evidence obtained by torture had been adequately excluded.'[20] And: 'SIAC understated or misunderstood the fundamental nature in convention law of the prohibition against the use of evidence obtained by torture.' (§45) And again: 'Our conclusion on the issue of evidence obtained by torture therefore remains that SIAC misdirected itself in law and its determination cannot stand.' (§70)

- 2009: A unanimous House of Lords reversed the decision of the Court of Appeal and reinstated SIAC's decision allowing Abu Qatada's deportation. In the words of Lord Hoffmann: 'In my opinion the Court of Appeal was wrong and SIAC was entitled to find that there was no breach of Article 6 in its application to a trial in a foreign state... There is in my opinion no authority for a rule that, in the context of the application of Article 6 to a foreign trial, the risk of the use of evidence obtained by torture necessarily amounts to a flagrant denial of justice.'[21]

- 2009: In accordance with this decision, the Home Secretary immediately served a deportation order on Abu Qatada, which however was not enforced pending his application to the European Court of Human Rights.

- 2012: The European Court of Human Rights found that, because there was a 'real risk' that two witnesses had been 'tortured into providing evidence against' Abu Qatada, 'there is a real risk that the applicant's retrial would amount to a flagrant denial of justice.'[22] Therefore: 'The Court finds that the applicant's deportation to Jordan would be a violation of Article 6 of the convention.' (§287)

- 2012: In spite of this, the Home Secretary again notified Abu Qatada that she intended to deport him two weeks later. Abu Qatada appealed against that decision under section 82(2)(k) of the Nationality Immigration & Asylum Act 2002. This appeal was again heard by SIAC, which this time found in his favour.[23] The key question, as before, was whether there was a 'risk' that statements obtained by torture would be used against Abu Qatada at his retrial in Jordan. Although the Secretary of State refused to revoke the deportation order, the order expressly stated that she 'does not seek to bypass the decision of the ECtHR'. (§17) And Counsel for the government went so far as to state 'that the decision letter was expressly drafted on the basis of the judgment of the Strasbourg Court and by reference to the test laid down by it' (§17) – the very test that the House of Lords had held to be wrong! The SIAC decision continued: 'In consequence, the Secretary of State accepts that if we were to find that the test identified by the Strasbourg Court has not been satisfied, we could or should allow the appellant's appeal on the basis that her discretion should have been exercised differently under section 86(3)(b) of the Nationality Immigration and Asylum Act 2002.' (§17) With this concession, the only way of preventing Abu Qatada from winning this appeal would have been by proving that no statements made under torture would be used against Abu Qatada. Although the Jordanian constitution had been amended to disallow torture or 'any statement extracted from a person under duress' (§69), SIAC concluded that the 'Secretary of State has not satisfied us that, on a retrial, there is no real risk' that evidence obtained by torture would be 'admitted probatively' against Abu Qatada. (§78)

- 2013: The Secretary of State appealed unsuccessfully to the Court of Appeal.[24] Once again, the central issue was said to be the risk that the evidence against Abu Qatada at a retrial in Jordan 'would include statements that have been obtained by torture and, if so, what effect this has on the lawfulness of his deportation'. (§1) There is no mention at all in this judgment of the 2009 decision of the House of Lords, which might have been thought to have cut the ground from under the whole idea of the relevance of torture evidence.

- 2014: After finally being deported back to Jordan, on 26 June 2014 Abu Qatada was acquitted of terrorist charges by a three-judge military court in Jordan, and on 24 September 2014 he was acquitted of further charges by a panel of civilian judges sitting in Jordan's State Security Court.

Recommendations

Here is my own suggested solution to the serious problem of UK human rights law, which agrees with some of the Conservative paper's suggestions but goes further by recognising the elephant in the room.

Human Rights and Responsibilities Bill

The government should amend the Human Rights Act (a) by changing its title to the Human Rights and Responsibilities Bill; (b) by repealing the pernicious sections 3 and 6; (c) by adding new sections laying down very clear ground rules for the courts to follow when interpreting and applying the ECHR; (d) by setting up parliamentary machinery to decide on any changes to human rights law, a power which must be taken away from the courts; and (e) by adding a list of responsibilities by which people will be expected to abide.

Judicial review

Judicial review is a procedure giving the High Court the power to quash (i.e. set aside) an administrative decision where the government body concerned has exceeded its powers. It does *not* give the court the right to substitute its own decision for that of the government body in question, which amounts to *usurping* the power of the government. Yet, in the past half century or so the courts have encroached more and more on the domain of the executive government – and even on that of the legislature, parliament. Successive governments have lamely stood by and watched while the courts have usurped powers that did not belong to them.

A major reform of judicial review is long overdue. In 2014 the government did at least introduce legislation to restrict the scope of judicial review. However, the government appears to have backed down after a defeat in the House of Lords on 27 October 2014. Lord Woolf, a former chief justice, warned: 'However carefully we legislate, it's dangerous to go down the line of telling the judges what they have got to do.' He added that it was necessary to 'safeguard judicial review' in order to avoid falling into 'the trap of an elective dictatorship' (column 959) (a phrase coined by Lord Hailsham in 1976). Needless to say, Lord Woolf omitted to mention the opposite danger of an *un*elected dictatorship of irremovable judges responsible to nobody. Also, 'telling the judges what they have got to do' is legislation – a function of parliament, not of the judiciary. For the judiciary to determine the scope of its own powers, which it has lamely been allowed to do by a succession of governments for the past half century or so, is an abdication of the democratic responsibility of both the government and parliament.

Constitutional Reform Act 2005

Section 3 of this act, which amounts to a total capitulation of the government to the judiciary, needs urgent amendment. Under the heading 'The guarantee of continued judicial independence', it provides that the government 'must uphold the continued independence of the judiciary'. On the face of it, this appears unobjectionable. Its 'independence' of course means, among other things, that the judiciary is not responsible to any body or institution. But that should not be allowed to mean 'irresponsibility' in a broader sense, of which, unfortunately, there has been a good deal of evidence in recent years. In addition, the independence of the judiciary from government interference must be balanced by the independence of the government and parliament from judicial meddling – which forms part of the concept of the separation of powers, which Lord Diplock famously declared to form the bedrock of the constitution: 'It cannot be too strongly emphasised that the British constitution, though largely unwritten, is firmly based on the separation of powers: parliament makes the laws, the judiciary interpret them'.[25] Separation of powers undoubtedly has a place in the British constitution, albeit not quite as central a place as it was accorded by Lord Diplock. The Constitutional Reform Act arose out of a so-called 'concordat' between the Chief Justice and the Lord Chancellor, which should indicate a compromise of some sort. But there is no sign of that in the Constitutional Reform Act. Instead, the judiciary has kept expanding the scope of its oversight of government decisions by means of judicial review, which calls for urgent pruning.

The elephant in the room

The Conservative Party is deluding itself if it thinks that, freed from the trammels of Strasbourg, the UK domestic courts will start interpreting convention rights on the basis of their plain, ordinary or literal meaning. The domestic courts are on an expansionist binge, which has never been checked by the government or parliament.

Continued failure to check this development will result not only in a serious weakening of national defences against terrorism and illegal immigration, but will also amount to a denial of democracy. Besides failing to check the judiciary's arrogation to itself of more and more powers, the government has not even tried to counter the increasingly vociferous arguments advanced in favour of this development. That task calls for urgent attention, which however is a major undertaking that will require a separate publication covering the following issues, among others:

- The rule of law *v* the rule of judges. Are judges allowed to legislate? If so, how does that square with the principle of the sovereignty of parliament? And if not, where does the borderline fall between legislation and interpretation? And who is to decide this issue?[26]

- What mechanism is there for law-abiding citizens to compel the government to protect them against crime, terrorism or illegal immigration?

- Amending the Human Rights Act by means of a new Human Rights and Responsibilities Bill (see above).

- The provisions of an amended Constitutional Reform Act clearly enunciating the principle of the sovereignty of parliament, clarifying the reciprocal nature and scope of the separation of powers and restricting the ambit of judicial review.

- Legislation to control the costs of civil litigation. The UK is the only country in the world where a claim worth, say, £30,000 may cost the loser legal fees of half a million pounds – which amounts to a denial of justice. A recent reform of civil litigation costs (on the basis of a lengthy report by a judge) has left this central problem unchecked. The government needs to take the bull by the horns and pass legislation to solve this serious problem – as in Germany, whose simple and eminently fair costs regime is statutory.[27]

● An ambitious new programme of parliamentary legislation. Most states of the United States, while remaining common law jurisdictions, have codified statutes covering all branches of law and procedure. The UK, by contrast, not only eschews codification but does not even have many areas of consolidated legislation. Instead, there is a welter of legislation on the same subject – like the innumerable employment laws, criminal justice acts and terrorism-related laws. Codification, or even consolidation, which would be a doddle to implement in this computer age of ours, would help to clarify the law, put the rule of law on a firmer footing and make it harder for the judges to take the law into their own hands.[28]

Conclusion

UK human rights law needs urgent attention. It has been hijacked by certain special interest groups, notably convicted prisoners (especially killers), illegal immigrants and terrorist suspects. But these groups cannot hijack the law by themselves. So who is responsible for this development? Many people, including the Conservative Party, point the finger at the Strasbourg Court. But, upon examination, this study shows that the real fault lies with the UK's own domestic courts, aided by a lame government too afraid to stand up to the judges.

It is only once the cause of the problem is correctly diagnosed that it can be successfully treated, and the treatment that I propose in this report certainly is drastic – and very different from that proposed by the Conservative Party or anybody else. At the time of writing, Andrew Parker, the head of MI5, has warned of a heightened risk of terrorist attacks on the UK and has called for new legal powers to combat this risk. It is time for the government to answer this call for action and to have the guts to resist the inevitable judicial opposition.

Notes

1 'Protecting Human Rights in the UK', Conservative Party: https://www.conservatives.com/~/media/Files/Downloadable%20Files/HUMAN_RIGHTS.pdf

2 Lord Irvine of Lairg, 'A British Interpretation of Convention Rights', lecture, 14 December 2011

3 (2009) 3 WLR 74, (2009) UKHL 28

4 (2004) UKHL 56

5 (1996) 23 EHRR 413

6 'The Brave New World of Sir John Laws', *Modern Law Review* 63 (2000) 159

7 Quoted by Lord Sumption in his Sultan Azlan Shah Lecture, 'The Limits of Law', 20 November 2013.

8 'Judicial & Political Decision-Making: The Uncertain Boundary', F.A. Mann Lecture, 2011

9 *R (Chester) v Secretary of State for Justice & McGeoch v Lord President* (2013) UKSC 63

10 (2012) 56 EHRR 63

11 (2005) 42 EHRR 849

12 (2010) 53 EHRR 710

13 (2012) 56 EHRR 663

14 (2014) ECHR 874

15 *Chester v Secretary of State for Justice* (2010) EWCA Civ 1439, at §2.

16 Lady Hale in *Chester*, § 88

17 BBC News, 23 March 2004: news.bbc.co.uk/1/hi/uk_politics/3562695.stm

18 SC/15/2005, 26 February 2007

19 Annex 3 to SIAC Judgment

20 (2008) EWCA Civ 290, §56

21 *OO (Jordan) v Secretary of State for the Home Department* (2009) UKHL 10; Othman v SSHD (2010) 2 AC 110, §201

22 *Othman (Abu Qatada) v UK* (Application No. 8139/09) §282)

23 Appeal No. SC/15/2005 – 12 November 2012; (2012) UKSIAC 15/2005_2

24 (2013) EWCA Civ 277

25 *Duport Steels v Sirs* (1980) 1 All ER 529

26 See Michael Arnheim, *Principles of the Common Law,* Duckworth, 2004

27 See Michael Arnheim, 'Costs – a missed opportunity?', *The Barrister,* 2010

28 See Michael Arnheim, *US Constitution for Dummies,* Wiley, 2009